SISK... ...S
...GOLD ST.
YREKA, CA 96097

D0605311

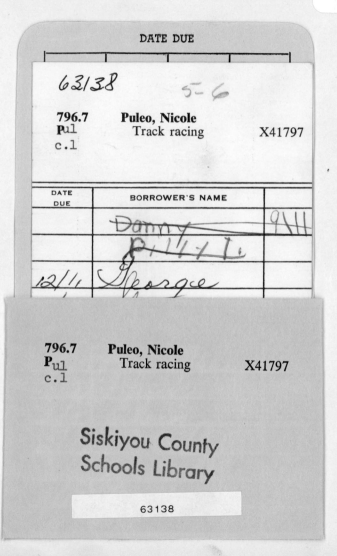

DATE DUE

63138   5-6

796.7   **Puleo, Nicole**
P̲u̲l   Track racing   X41797
c.1

DATE DUE	BORROWER'S NAME	
	~~Danny~~	9/11
12/11	George	

796.7   **Puleo, Nicole**
P̲u̲l   Track racing   X41797
c.1

Siskiyou County
Schools Library

63138

TRACK RACING

The Lerner Racing Series
Ronald J. Larsen, Series Editor
Mark Dillon, Editorial Consultant
Peg Sanford, Photo Editor
Victoria Hakala, Artist

63138

The Racing Books

TRACK RACING

NICOLE PULEO

Siskiyou County
Schools Library

Lerner Publications Company ■ Minneapolis, Minnesota

ACKNOWLEDGMENTS: The illustrations are reproduced through the courtesy of: pp. 4, 13, 27, Ford Motor Company, Educational Affairs Department; pp. 7, 31, 35, 39, 43, National Association for Stock Car Auto Racing, Inc.; pp. 9, 19, 21, 23, 47, Indianapolis Motor Speedway Corporation; p. 11, Pocono International Raceway; p. 15, STP Corporation; p. 17, E.I. Du Pont De Nemours & Company; p. 25, United States Auto Club; pp. 29, 33, Thomas B. Furr, Jr.; p. 37, Dennis Popp; p. 45, Minnesota State Fair.

LIBRARY OF CONGRESS CATALOGING IN PUBLICATION DATA

Puleo, Nicole.
    Track racing.

    (The Racing Books)
    SUMMARY: Describes stock cars, sports cars, hot rods, and other race cars that compete in such track races as the Indianapolis 500 and the Daytona 500.

    1. Automobile racing—United States—Juvenile literature. [1. Automobile racing] I. Title.

GV1033.P84   796.7'2   72-5419
ISBN 0-8225-0405-7

Copyright © 1973 by Lerner Publications Company

All rights reserved. International copyright secured. Manufactured in the United States of America. Published simultaneously in Canada by J. M. Dent & Sons Ltd., Don Mills, Ontario.

International Standard Book Number: 0-8225-0405-7
Library of Congress Catalog Card Number: 72-5419

Second Printing 1974

INTRODUCTION

No other machine has changed our lives more than the automobile. In the time between the introduction of the first "horseless carriage" and the development of today's fast-moving, high-powered models, the car has become an essential part of daily life. The automobile and the new superhighways designed for it have given us more freedom to travel than we have ever known before. Partly because of the car, our cities are emptying, as people move to the suburbs and drive to the cities for work. And, as everyone knows, the millions of cars on the road have polluted our air and endangered our lives (more than 3 million injuries and 55,000 deaths result from car accidents each year in the United States alone). But in spite of the problems and dangers it presents, the automobile will probably be with us for a long time.

Here are some staggering statistics. By the end of 1971, a grand total of over 285 million motor vehicles had been produced in the United States. Over 100 million of them, including more than 90 million passenger vehicles, were registered in 1971 for highway use by the country's 100 million licensed drivers. One-sixth of all the businesses in the United States are involved in the automobile trade, and one out of every four households owns more than one car.

To some people, the car is just a simple necessity, like a vacuum cleaner or a refrigerator. But to race-car drivers, it is practically their whole reason for living. Each year, auto races in the United States attract a paid attendance of over 50 million people. Horse racing, which has the advantage of legal betting, is the only sport that claims a higher attendance than auto racing.

Some experts predict that auto racing is going to get even more popular, becoming the number one spectator sport of the 1970s. This will almost certainly happen in the United States, where people have money to spend on cars and racing. But even in countries like Argentina and Russia, where the automobile is a luxury, motor racing is becoming more popular all the time.

In the United States, auto racing means big investments, big purses, big promotions, and big crowds. Until recently, motor racing in this country was restricted mainly to *track racing*, a type of racing which is native to the United States. In track racing, cars run laps around oval tracks. These paved or dirt tracks have long straightaways and curves that are sometimes banked. Another popular kind of auto racing is *road racing*. Although this kind of racing has been popular in Europe for a long time, it has become widespread in America only during the last few years. Road races were originally run on public roads, but today they are usually run on special road tracks. Like public roads, these irregularly shaped tracks have several sharp corners, curves, and grades.

Exciting track races like the Daytona 500 attract more fans every year.

Track racing came naturally to Americans, who have always been drawn to competitive sports. When the first cars came out, they were raced on the horse-racing tracks found at fairgrounds throughout the country. In these early days of auto racing, "horseless carriages" were occasionally pitted against horses in special track races, and the cars didn't always win!

The "horseless carriage" has come a long way since the early 1900s, and horses wouldn't stand a chance against the ultra-fast autos in a track race like the Indianapolis 500. This world-famous race is held by the United States Auto Club (USAC), one of the four major organizations that sanction (give approval to) auto races in this country. USAC, together with the National Association for Stock Car Auto Racing (NASCAR), controls most of the track racing in the United States. The Sports Car Club of America (SCCA) sponsors most of the road racing, and the National Hot Rod Association (NHRA) runs most of the drag racing.

Thousands of spectators watch the Indianapolis 500—the most famous auto race of them all.

THE CHAMPIONSHIP TRAIL

The United States Auto Club's most important series of track races is known as the Championship Trail. There are 12 races in this series, and they are all run on paved oval tracks. In each race, the winner and runners-up are awarded money and points. At the end of the year, the driver who has won the most points becomes the USAC Driving Champion.

Organized in 1909, the Championship Trail has provided racing fans with many exciting races through the years. Although the series once included anywhere from 20 to 25 races (including a number of road races), it was reduced to 12 track races in 1971. USAC took this action in order to reduce the pressure on the drivers, to increase the size of the purses, and to improve the quality of the races.

The most famous race in the Championship Trail is the Indianapolis 500, which is held at Indianapolis Motor Speedway on Memorial Day weekend. Besides the 500-mile Indianapolis race, two other 500-mile races are included in the championship series. One of them, the Pocono 500, is held on Independence Day at Pocono International Raceway in Pennsylvania. The other, the California 500, is run at Ontario Motor Speedway in Southern California during the Labor Day weekend. Together, these three races are referred to as the "triple crown" of auto racing. The other nine championship races are shorter, ranging from 150 to 300 miles.

Cars take a warm-up lap behind an official pace car at Pocono International Raceway in Pennsylvania.

CHAMPIONSHIP CARS

The cars that compete in the Championship Trail are called championship, or "Indy," cars. Many different kinds of engines are used in championship cars, ranging from powerful overhead camshaft (OHC) engines to less powerful "stock-block" engines, which are those built to passenger car specifications. Although they need not be, most of the engines used in Indy cars are "supercharged." A "supercharger" is a blower that increases an engine's power by forcing air into its cylinders at a greater pressure than that exerted by the atmosphere. Because supercharged engines are more powerful than nonsupercharged ones, they use gas more quickly and get more revolutions per minute (rpm).

In order to promote fair competition, USAC equalizes the power of the engines used in championship cars by enforcing strict "formulas," or sets of rules and specifications. These formulas limit the size of the engines according to their type: the more powerful an engine, the smaller its size must be. Engine size, measured in cubic inches (ci) or cubic centimeters (cc), is the amount of space inside the cylinders. Following are the size limits on the four types of engines used in championship cars: (1) supercharged OHC engines—161.7 ci; (2) supercharged stock-block engines—203.4 ci; (3) nonsupercharged OHC engines—256.3 ci; and (4) nonsupercharged stock-block engines—320.4 ci.

Equipped with powerful supercharged engines, championship cars can travel at fantastic speeds.

Most championship cars run with the first kind of engine—a supercharged OHC engine up to 161.7 cubic inches in size. Since these engines are usually equipped with "turbochargers" (special kinds of superchargers), "turbocharged" is really a better term for them than "supercharged." While the unmodified engine of a large family car can generate about 350 horsepower, the turbocharged engine of an Indy car can generate over 800 horsepower!

For a few years, some championship cars were powered by a special kind of engine, called the turbine engine. In this engine, the hot gases produced by burning the fuel are used to run a turbine—a series of rotating blades arranged like those in a windmill or a water wheel. In 1967 Andy Granatelli, president of the STP Corporation, entered his STP Turbocar in the Indianapolis 500. It was a funny-looking, bright red car, with the engine on the left side of the driver. Driven by the well-known driver Parnelli Jones, the turbocar took an early lead in the race. But within 10 miles of the finish line, a small six-dollar transmission part broke down, taking the car out of the race.

In spite of this defeat, Granatelli did not lose faith in the turbine engine. Instead, he entered three turbocars in the 1968 Indianapolis 500. One was in the lead near the end of the race, but again a minor part broke down and kept the car from finishing.

Andy Granatelli's famous Turbocar, 1967

No turbine-engine cars were entered in the Indianapolis 500 after 1968. This was not because of discouragement over the bad luck of the earlier turbocars, but because of a change in USAC's rules. The new rules did not prohibit the use of turbine engines, but they severely restricted their size. Thus it was no longer practical to build Indy cars with turbine engines, and the turbocars quickly died out.

Like the engines, the bodies of championship cars are subject to rigid formulas. Indy cars are single-seat, cigar-shaped vehicles built with rear engines, open cockpits, and "open wheels," which means they have no fenders. Nor do they have headlights, taillights, bumpers, or doors. But they do have a small windscreen, a "roll bar" (a tubular steel frame that protects the driver in case of an accident), and huge, widely spaced tires. Championship cars can be no longer than 16 feet, and they must weigh at least 1,350 pounds without fuel or driver (most family cars weigh twice this much).

Championship-car drivers are surrounded by fuel—up to 75 gallons of it. The fuel is

Face masks, gloves, and fire-resistant suits are worn by all Indy-car drivers.

carried in strong rubber tanks, called "bladders," that resist puncture. Indy cars are not powered by regular pump gasoline, but by a special blend of two exotic fuels, nitromethane and methanol.

Because of the danger of fires, all championship cars are equipped with fire extinguishers. As a further precaution against fires and accidents, all championship-car drivers are required to wear protective gear. This gear includes a firesuit, a face mask, flame-resistant underwear, a sturdy helmet, gloves, and boots.

THE INDIANAPOLIS 500

Every aspiring race-car driver dreams of someday competing in the Indianapolis 500, the only million-dollar auto race in the world. This spectacular Championship Trail event is held each Memorial Day weekend at Indianapolis Motor Speedway, also known as "the Speedway." Opened in 1909, the Speedway was the first paved oval track built for auto racing. Many other oval tracks have been built since, but the Indianapolis Motor Speedway has remained the most famous.

The Indianapolis 500 is considered to be *the* track race of the year—the one with the most prestige, the most money, and the most publicity. "The 500," as it is called by racing fans, consists of 200 laps around the Speedway's 2.5-mile course, for a total of 500 miles. Each year, over 250,000 fans flood the Indy

grandstands and infield to take in the big race.

The two weeks before the Indianapolis race are a busy time at the Speedway. Drivers practice to get the "feel" of the course and to decide exactly how they will take each of the Speedway's four left turns (since the Indy 500 is a 200-lap race, the drivers will have to make a total of 800 turns). Experienced drivers will tell you that each of the Speedway's four turns is different in some little, but important, way.

After the practice sessions are over, the drivers enter the qualifying trials. In order to qualify for the Indianapolis 500, a driver must run four timed laps around the Speedway, for a total of 10 miles. Of the 70 to 90 drivers who compete in the qualifying runs, only the fastest 33 make it to the big race.

Aerial view of Indianapolis Motor Speedway

The qualifier with the best speed gets to start the Indy 500 in the "pole position," the number one position in the starting lineup. Just before the start of the Indy 500, the 33 qualifiers line up in rows of three, in the order of their qualifying times (the fastest 3 qualifiers are in the first row, the next 3 fastest are in the second row, and so on). The driver in the pole position is the one closest to the inside of the track and in the first row of cars. He is said to be "sitting on the pole" because his position gives him the lead into the first turn of the race.

The average speeds reached during the 10-mile qualifying trials at Indy are almost always higher than those reached during the actual 500-mile race. In 1972, lap speeds during the Indy race averaged about 155 miles per hour (mph), while those in the qualifying runs averaged about 185 mph.

Bobby Unser, the fastest qualifier, established a new Speedway record by averaging 195.9 mph during his 10-mile qualifying run.

Once the 33 fastest qualifiers have been selected, they eagerly await the day of the race. Finally, the big day arrives. The "running start" of the Indianapolis 500 is one of the most thrilling events in the world of racing. After all the cars have taken their qualifying positions, the president of the Speedway says over the loudspeaker, "Gentlemen, start your engines!" The cars then take two or three slow laps around the track behind an official pace car. This allows the engines to warm up and gets the cars tightly spaced together, still in the proper order. When the cars are lined up well, the pace car leaves the track, and the pace is set by the car in the pole position. Then, without warning, the green flag is waved and the race is on!

The parade lap of the Indy 500

With the roaring sound of over 20,000 horsepower, the cars rip down the Speedway. It is not unusual for an Indy car to travel at a speed of 200 mph when covering one of the course's two long straightaways (each one is five-eighths of a mile long). Five hundred miles and just over three hours after the start of the race, a black-and-white checkered flag waves over the new winner. Usually, less than half of the 33 qualifiers are still on the track at the finish. Engine problems and other mechanical difficulties account for the high dropout rate.

In 1972, the Indy 500 had a purse of over $1 million. The winner, Mark Donohue, received over $215,000. Close to $100,000 went to Al Unser, who placed second in the race. Together, the three 500-mile races in the Championship Trail pay out more than $2 million to winning drivers each year. The other nine track races in the championship series pay a total of about $1 million. For world-famous drivers like Mario Andretti, A. J. Foyt, Al Unser and his brother Bobby, Championship Trail racing means big money.

Mark Donohue, the winner of the 1972 Indianapolis 500

OTHER USAC RACES

In addition to the Championship Trail races, USAC also sanctions races for dirt-track cars, sprint cars, and midget cars. Each of these racing divisions offers something different, and each has its own group of dedicated fans.

As the name suggests, dirt-track racers are cars that run on dirt tracks. These open-wheel cars are about the same size as Indy cars, but their engines are in front, not at the rear. Dirt-track cars are heavier than Indy cars and are designed to race on dirt tracks faster than Indy cars can. The dirt tracks used for USAC's races must be at least one mile long. Because more and more dirt tracks are being replaced by paved tracks, dirt-track racing is in danger of extinction. But the rugged sport is still a favorite of some fans and drivers, and USAC is taking steps to develop a championship program for it.

Sprint cars are open-wheel, front-engine racers like dirt-track cars, only they are smaller and less powerful. The United States Auto Club sanctions about 35 sprint-car races throughout the country each year. Most of these races are quite short, consisting of 30 laps around a half-mile track (both paved and dirt tracks are used for sprint-car racing). The speeds in sprint races reach a top of about 120 mph—not all that fast compared to Indy 500 speeds of over 200 mph. Nevertheless, the small tracks and the fearless drivers make sprint-car racing one of the most exciting categories of motor racing.

Midget cars, as you might guess, are even smaller than sprint cars. In fact, these front-engine, open-wheel racers are miniature versions of dirt-track cars. Because of the fierce competition and relatively slow speeds, midget racing is considered about the best training a race-car driver can get. Each year USAC sanctions between 60 and 70 midget-car races, most of which are held on quarter-mile tracks. Midget racing is so competitive and exciting that many experienced race-car drivers participate in it whenever they can.

Sprint cars compete in a USAC-approved race.

STOCK-CAR RACING

Native to the United States, stock-car racing is the most popular kind of track racing in this country. In fact, it is the most popular of *all* types of U.S. motor racing, attracting the most drivers, the most cars, and the most spectators. While stock-car racing is particularly strong in the South, it is also gaining much strength in the Midwest. During the summer months, stock-car events are becoming almost as much a part of the scene as mosquitoes.

Some authorities claim that stock-car racing began during the early days of moonshine deliveries in the southeastern United States. Drivers carrying the illegally distilled liquor needed well-tuned, powerful cars to escape from government agents. When making their deliveries, they learned to race down back-country roads at breakneck speeds. Although their work was risky, the bootleggers enjoyed driving at daredevil speeds and took pride in their powerful cars. It was only a matter of time, then, before they began challenging each other to informal stock-car races.

Although bootleggers were important to stock-car racing, they were not the only ones who helped develop the sport. Even the earliest automobile owners liked to see how their cars compared to their neighbors' cars. So they staged motor contests on deserted country roads or in vacant fields. As the sport became more popular, weekend mechanics tried to get more horsepower out of their cars' engines. By 1947, when the National Association for Stock Car Auto Racing was formed, stock-car racing had become one of the South's most popular sports. Today, the sport draws millions of participants and fans from all over the United States. Stock-car racing has come a long way!

Stock cars take one of the turns at Daytona International Speedway.

THE CARS

Actually, "stock car" is a misleading name for most of the cars that compete in professional stock-car races. The only reason they are called "stock cars" is because they look like the "stock," or "ordinary," passenger cars that Americans drive every day. The body of a stock-car racer is taken from the assembly line where regular cars are made, but from then on, it gets special treatment. First, the bare, unpainted steel body is reinforced inside with steel bars to strengthen it and to form a "roll cage" to protect the driver. Then the doors, fenders, grille sections, seats, windows, and other furnishings are added by the race-car builders. For the front and back windows, the builders use heavy shatterproof glass.

A stock-car racer has no taillights or head-lights, and its doors are welded shut for added body strength (the drivers crawl in and out through the window). In cars made especially for oval-track racing, where all the turns are to the left, a headrest is attached to the right-hand side of the driver's seat. The headrest is positioned to the driver's right side because all of the left turns in an oval track race constantly push the driver's head to the right. (With a heavy helmet on, a race-car driver really gets tired of holding his head upright, and the headrest makes it easier for him.) The other parts of the car, including the frame and brakes, are carefully strengthened for extra wear and safety. All of these improvements make stock-car racing one of the safest of all types of motor racing.

Although they look like ordinary passenger cars, stock cars are much faster and sturdier.

The engine in a stock car isn't really "stock" either. Following the formulas established by NASCAR and other stock-car organizations, the engine builder makes every part specially. His measurements for each piece of the engine are precise, and his materials are of the finest quality. The end result is an engine that can generate tremendous speeds for long periods of time without breaking down. Ordinary engines simply could not take the stresses of a long race at high speeds.

Like the engines, the tires used for professional stock cars are quite special. About 12 inches wide, they are made of compounds that give the car greater traction than ordinary tires. Even so, one pair of these sturdy tires cannot last through a long race.

Thus the stock cars found in professional track races are a far cry from the stock cars most Americans drive. For this reason, "stock-appearing" is a much better term than "stock" for these professional race cars. But to most racing fans, what the cars are called doesn't really matter. What *does* matter is speed and excitement, and at stock-car races, there is plenty of both.

The rugged tires used for stock
cars are designed to take the
wear and tear of ultra-fast racing.

NASCAR

Although USAC sanctions some stock-car races, the National Association for Stock Car Auto Racing is the largest sanctioning body for stock-car racing in the country. Formed in 1947, NASCAR sanctions over 1,200 events each year. These events, which are held on more than 90 tracks throughout the country, boast a total purse of $5.5 million.

In order to encourage fair competition, NASCAR has established a whole network of stock-car racing divisions. This network includes the Grand National division, the Grand American Series, the Late Model Sportsman division, the Modified division, and the Hobby division. Each of these divisions is for a specific type of stock car, and each is governed by its own set of rules.

NASCAR's fastest and most prestigious division of stock-car racing is the Grand National. This division is for steel-bodied sedans made in America during the three most recent production years. Mercurys, Fords, Plymouths, Chevrolets, and Dodges are included in the Grand National division. Although the body of a Grand National car can be modified for safety, the only thing that can be added to the body itself is a 1.5-inch spoiler, or air deflector. Grand National cars must weigh at least 3,800 pounds, and they run on nonsupercharged stock-block engines. The maximum engine size for a Grand National car is 430 ci. Equipped with these powerful engines, Grand National cars attain fantastic speeds of over 200 mph.

Stock cars compete in one of NASCAR's Grand National races.

Over 50 races are included in the Grand National division, with each race averaging a purse of about $35,000. The 10 longest Grand National races are held on NASCAR's five greatest speedways. The longest of these is Florida's 2.5-mile Daytona International Speedway. This speedway hosts the Daytona 500 in February and the Firecracker 400 on the Fourth of July. Darlington International Raceway in South Carolina is the oldest of the speedways. It hosts the Rebel 400 in spring and the Southern 500 on Labor Day. The Atlanta 500 (spring) and the Dixie 500 (summer) are both held at Atlanta International Speedway in Georgia. Charlotte Motor Speedway in North Carolina holds the World 600 in spring and the National 500 in fall. And North Carolina Motor Speedway—NASCAR's newest speedway—holds the Carolina 500 in spring and the American 500 in fall. Most of the other Grand National races are about 100 miles long and are run on half- and quarter-mile oval tracks.

The "sporty sedans," such as the Mustang, Camaro, Javelin, and Barracuda, are not large enough to race in the Grand Nationals. They have their own NASCAR division called the Grand American Series. Like Grand National cars, Grand American cars must be from the three most recent production years, and their bodies may be altered only for safety reasons. The minimum weight for these cars is 3,200 pounds, or 700 pounds less than that of Grand National cars. Grand American cars run on stock-block engines up to 305 ci in size. Although some of the Grand American races are run on road courses, most of them are run on oval tracks.

Daytona International Speedway

Older, less powerful cars compete in the three remaining NASCAR divisions: Late Model Sportsman, Modified, and Hobby. Each year NASCAR sanctions over 1,000 events for these three divisions alone. These races do not have very large purses, but they provide excitement for fans and good training for beginning race-car drivers.

The Late Model Sportsman division is for sedans produced in the 10-year period ending three years before the current season (for the 1972 season, the period covers 1959 to 1969). Very few modifications of the body or engine are allowed in this division, but the engine size can be up to 430 ci.

In the Modified division, almost any modifications of the cars are permitted—even supercharged engines may be used. Any car made between 1935 and the production year ending three years before the current season (1935 to 1969 for the 1972 season) may compete in the Modified division. For the Hobby division—the slowest of all NASCAR's divisions—a car must be between 10 and 25 years old. Since Hobby cars are relatively inexpensive, they are truly for amateurs who love racing but don't want to spend a small fortune on it.

A close-up of a Late Model Sportsman engine

To minimize the possibility of fires, NASCAR does not permit the use of large gasoline tanks in any of the cars that compete in its races. A 22-gallon tank is the largest the rules allow. Since even the fastest cars get only six or seven miles to a gallon, pit stops during the long-distance Grand National races have to be pretty frequent. However, top pit crews can change two tires, fill the tank, clean the windshield, and even give the driver a cool drink in about 25 seconds! All these things are done by five men—the most the rules allow. In long, grueling races, the speed and efficiency of the driver's pit crew can make the difference between winning and losing.

Each year over 100,000 spectators watch the Daytona 500, the most famous of NASCAR's Grand National races. This mid-winter event is held at Daytona International Speedway in Daytona Beach, Florida. Opened in 1959, the 2.5-mile speedway is the longest and fastest oval track on NASCAR's racing circuit.

As in most stock-car races, qualifying runs for the Daytona 500 take place the week before the race. On the day of the race, the cars with the fastest qualifying times line up in rows of two (the two fastest qualifiers are in the first row, the next two fastest are in the second row, and so on). As in the Indianapolis 500, the driver with the best qualifying speed gets to start the race in the pole position—the position in the first row of cars that is closest to the inside of the track.

Drivers have to make many pit stops during a long race like the Daytona 500.

The start of the Daytona 500 is much like the start of the Indy 500. One minute before the race, the starter signals the drivers to start their engines. After the starter is sure that everyone is ready, he gives a signal for the pace lap to begin. During the pace lap, he checks to see that the cars are tightly spaced together and are moving at a constant, slow speed. Satisfied with the speed and formation of the cars, the starter suddenly waves the green flag, which means, "The course is clear. Start!" Now that the race has begun, the cars can pass each other in attempts to gain a better position. But if a driver tries to pass another car *before* the green flag has been waved, he runs the risk of either being disqualified or of being sent to the pit to stay there for a minute.

Besides the green flag, many other types of flags are used during the Daytona 500 and other stock-car races, and each one tells the drivers something different. While the solid yellow flag means, "Take care, danger, no passing," the yellow flag with vertical red stripes means, "Take care. Oil has been spilled or a slippery condition exists somewhere on the road." The solid red flag means, "Stop immediately. Clear the circuit.

RACING FLAGS

Start—course is clear

Caution—no passing

Stop—course blocked

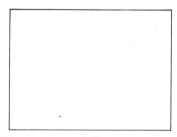

Take care—ambulance on course

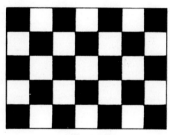

Finish

Pull into pits

Give way

The race has been stopped." When the blue flag with a diagonal yellow stripe is held motionless, it means, "Another competitor is following you very closely," but when the same flag is waved, it means, "A faster competitor is trying to overtake you. Give way." A white flag means, "There is an ambulance or service vehicle on the circuit. Take care." An open black flag means, "Complete the lap you are now on. Then stop at your pit." But if the black flag is rolled up, it means, "Warning—you are driving in an unsafe or improper manner. If you continue, you will be given a black flag." A black flag with an orange circle in the center means, "There is something wrong with your car. Go to your pit at reduced speed." And, of course, the black-and-white checkered flag means, "Congratulations, you have finished the race!"

The first driver to get the checkered flag at the Daytona 500 wins not only the race, but also a great deal of money. In 1972, the Daytona 500 had a total purse of about $180,000. A. J. Foyt, who won the race with a record-breaking average speed of 161 miles per hour, was awarded close to $40,000. The second-place driver, Charlie Glotzbach, won about $15,000.

A. J. Foyt (left), the winner of the 1972 Daytona 500, with car-owner Leonard Wood (right)

OTHER STOCK-CAR ORGANIZATIONS

The Automobile Racing Club of America (ARCA), which was called the Midwest Association for Race Cars from 1952 to 1963, is the second-largest sanctioning body for stock-car racing in the United States. It runs four divisions of races—the National Championship Stock Cars, the Late Model Sportsman, the Hobby Stock Cars, and the Figure Eight. ARCA's most important series of races is the National Championship Stock Cars. This division is for one- and two-year-old stock cars made in America. The races in this division alone have an annual purse of more than $1 million.

The International Motor Contest Association (IMCA) is another organization for stock-car races. IMCA was established in 1915 and is the oldest sanctioning body for auto races in the United States. A nonprofit organization, it is owned by various state fairs around the country. IMCA's annual purse for all its events is about $250,000. This may not seem like a very large purse for car racing, but since most of the money comes from the race drivers' admission fees, it is actually a rather impressive sum.

This IMCA stock-car race is held at the Minnesota State Fair before thousands of spectators.

CONCLUSION

Motor racing offers plenty of thrills to the spectators and plenty of money to the winners. But it is probably not the money that attracts serious drivers. More likely, it is the challenge and danger of the sport. As crowded living conditions force us to retreat more and more into our safe little cocoons, the risks and dangers, the freedom and excitement of car racing will continue to attract both drivers and spectators.

Some people have a theory that spectators are drawn to the race track by the desire to see someone killed in a crash. Certainly, there are some people like this, anxious to see a disaster. But most fans are attracted more by the *potential* dangers of racing at fantastic speeds than by any desire for an actual mishap. To watch skilled drivers "turn it on" during the Indy 500 or the Daytona 500 is truly an exhilarating experience. For serious fans, there's nothing to match car racing.

A checkered flag waves down the winner of an important track race.

THE RACING BOOKS

DRAG RACING
ICE RACING
MOTORCYCLE RACING
ROAD RACING
SNOWMOBILE RACING
TRACK RACING
AMERICAN RACE CAR DRIVERS
INTERNATIONAL RACE CAR DRIVERS
THE INDIANAPOLIS 500

*We specialize in publishing quality books for
young people. For a complete list please write:*

Lerner Publications Company
241 First Avenue North, Minneapolis, Minnesota 55401

SISKIYOU CO. SUPT. SCHOOLS
LIBRARY
609 S. GOLD ST.
YREKA, CA 96097